# Twenty to Make

# Crocheted Hearts

## May Corfield

Search Press

First published in 2015

Search Press Limited
Wellwood, North Farm Road,
Tunbridge Wells, Kent TN2 3DR

Reprinted 2017

Print ISBN: 978-1-78221-063-4
ebook ISBN: 978-1-78126-220-7

You are invited to view the author's work on
Facebook at: May Corfield Crochet

Suppliers
If you have difficulty in obtaining any of the
materials and equipment mentioned in this book,
then please visit the Search Press website for
details of suppliers: www.searchpress.com

Printed in China through Asia Pacific Offset

### Dedication
*In memory of my lovely Mum, who taught
me to crochet and encouraged all needle skills
and creativity.*

## Crochet Abbreviations

The abbreviations listed below are the most
frequently used terms in the book. Any
special abbreviations in a crochet pattern are
explained on the relevant project page.

| US | UK |
|---|---|
| sl st (slip stitch) | sl st (slip stitch) |
| ch st (chain stitch) | ch st (chain stitch) |
| ch sp (chain space) | ch sp (chain space) |
| sc (single crochet) | dc (double crochet) |
| hdc (half double crochet) | htr (half treble crochet) |
| dc (double crochet) | tr (treble crochet) |
| tr (treble crochet) | dtr (double treble crochet) |
| dtr (double treble crochet) | trtr (triple treble crochet) |
| trtr (triple treble) | qtr (quadruple treble) |
| skip | miss |
| yrh (yarn round hook) | yrh (yarn round hook) |
| beg (beginning) | beg (beginning) |
| rep (repeat) | rep (repeat) |
| sp/s (space(s)) | sp/s (space(s)) |
| tbl (through back loop) | tbl (through back loop) |

# Contents

# Introduction

The heart has been a universally popular and much-loved motif in art for centuries. It transfers very well to crochet, and I have tried to use it in as wide a range of projects as possible. I have included a rug, a pincushion, a pillow, some coasters, a Christmas heart, a brooch and a hair clip, among others.

The reason that the crocheted heart is fascinating is that there are many different ways to construct this pretty design. The 'back and forth' design, which I have used for the Long Tall Heart, the Rug and the Coasters, is very straightforward and can be embellished by the addition of a decorative edging in a contrasting colour. The Chunky Pillow uses a spiral design and requires the use of a stitch marker, to keep track of where you are.

The 'square with added lobes' has been used for the Valentine heart, the Nautical Heart and the Heart Charm and is very versatile. Another construction is the 'in the round' type, which has been used for the Jewellery Box, the Heart String, the Brooch and the Snowflakes. Crocheted hearts can also be described in filet crochet, as in the Filet Heart, or using granny squares. The great thing is that they all look completely different, which is really the beauty of crocheting hearts – but they are also very addictive!

The projects are all easy and fairly quick to make. I have used a variety of crochet stitches, all of which can be managed with ease by competent beginners and seasoned crocheters alike.

# Crochet know-how

## US and UK crochet terminology

The names for basic crochet stitches differ in the UK and the US. In all patterns, US terms are given first, followed by the UK terms in brackets – for example, US single crochet is written as sc *(UKdc)*, and US double crochet as dc *(UKtr)*.

## Yarn

I have used a wide variety of yarns for these projects, from fine crochet cotton to super chunky jersey yarn, and all weights in between. It is not essential to use the same yarn; all of these projects can be produced with a similar yarn – just make sure that you check the weight and yardage of yarn you choose against the ones used in this book to ensure you have enough yarn to finish your projects. Bear in mind that, for the smaller projects, you can use yarn that you already have in your stash.

## Crochet hooks

Crochet hooks are made from aluminium, steel, plastic, bamboo and wood and there are many different types. I prefer to work with an aluminium hook that has an ergonomic, cushioned handle, which I find very comfortable and easy to use. Experiment with different types to find the one that suits you best. It is important to use one which gives you good control, as well as being easy on your hands.

## Tension

I have not given a specific tension for these projects, as they are accessories and the size they turn out to be is not crucial. Bear in mind that if you use a lighter or heavier weight of yarn than the one specified, your item will be correspondingly smaller or larger. With larger items, take note of the yardage specified to make sure you have enough yarn to complete your project.

## Other materials

I have used a range of beads and accessories for these projects, all of which are easily available from craft suppliers. From seed beads to larger plastic beads, faux pearls and brass bell beads to heart-shaped buttons, some were bought, some donated and others were in my craft stash or my daughter's necklace-making kit. You can be creative and use whatever comes to hand to make your own projects unique.

## Blocking

The purpose of blocking is to finish off a piece of crochet, make it look regular and professional, and 'set' the stitches. Flat pieces of crochet often benefit from blocking, especially if they are liable to curl at the edges. All you need is a large piece of foam about 1in (2.5cm) thick, a clean towel, a can of spray starch (or spray bottle filled with warm water) and some pins.

**1** Lay the towel over the piece of foam.

**2** Place your piece of crochet in the middle of the towel and spray it with the starch or warm water so it is saturated.

**3** Now pin out your crochet carefully to the shape you want. You may need to use a ruler if you want a shape of exact dimensions.

**4** Leave it to dry, making sure it remains undisturbed.

**5** Once it is completely dry, unpin your crochet and it will be a nice, flat regular shape.

# Chunky Pillow

## Materials:

2 x 100g balls Cygnet Seriously Chunky in Bluebell, 100g/48m/52yd, or a similar chunky yarn

Toy stuffing

## Tools:

US size 16/12mm crochet hook

Stitch marker

Large-eyed needle

## Finished size:

From bottom point to centre top between lobes: 8⅝in (22cm)

## Instructions:

This heart is worked from the bottom point.

Ch 2 and work 4 sc (UKdc) in second ch from hook.

Now work in a spiral, making *1 sc (UKdc), 2 sc (UKdc) in next st*, and rep until you have 24 sts; place stitch marker in the last st.

Next round: work 1 sc (UKdc) in each st around. Replace marker in the last st.

Next round: *1 sc (UKdc) in next 2 sts, 2 sc (UKdc) in next st*, rep until you have 32 sts. Place marker.

Next 3 rounds: work 1 sc (UKdc) in each st around, moving marker up as you make each round.

Next round: *1 sc (UKdc) in next 2 sts, 2 sc (UKdc) in next st* until you have 40 sts. Move marker.

Next 3 rounds: work 1 sc (UKdc) in each st around, moving marker up as you make each round.

### To make the first lobe:

Keep using the stitch marker to mark the beginning of a new round.

Next round: sc (UKdc) in next 10 sts, skip 20 sts, sc (UKdc) in last 10 sts (20 sts).

Next round: work 1 sc (UKdc) in each st around (20 sts).

**Next round: sc (UKdc) in next 7 sts, [sc (UKdc)2tog x 3], sc (UKdc) in next 7 sts (17 sts).

Next round: sc (UKdc) in next 5 sts, [sc (UKdc)2tog x 3], sc (UKdc) in next 6 sts (14 sts).

Next round: sc (UKdc) in next 4 sts, [sc (UKdc)2tog x 3], sc (UKdc) in next 4 sts (11 sts).

Next round: sc (UKdc) in next 2 sts, [sc (UKdc)2tog x 3], sc (UKdc) in next 3 sts (8 sts).

Cut a long tail and thread onto a large-eyed tapestry needle. Catch the front loop of each rem st, going from inside outwards. Then pull the yarn taut to close the hole at the top of the lobe and push the yarn through the closed hole to the inside of the heart and leave it there.***

### To make the second lobe:

Rejoin the yarn to the outer stitch at the edge of the heart, ch 1 and work 1 sc (UKdc) into each st (20 sts).

There will be a small gap in the sts in the centre of the heart where the two lobes meet. Now is the time to close this up by inserting a few sts using a spare length of yarn and the large-eyed tapestry needle.

Next round: sc *(UKdc)* in each st around (20 sts).

Now stuff the heart, making sure to get the stuffing into the bottom point using your crochet hook or a pencil and filling the completed lobe. For the remaining part of the second lobe, keep adding more stuffing as you go, making sure to pack enough in just before you close the second lobe.

Now follow pattern for first lobe from ** to ***.

# Jewellery Box

**Materials:**

Small amount of jersey yarn in turquoise

1 x 1200g spool/120m/131yd

**Tools:**

US size 15/10mm crochet hook

**Finished size:**

From bottom point to centre top between lobes: 6½in (16.5cm); depth 1¼in (3cm)

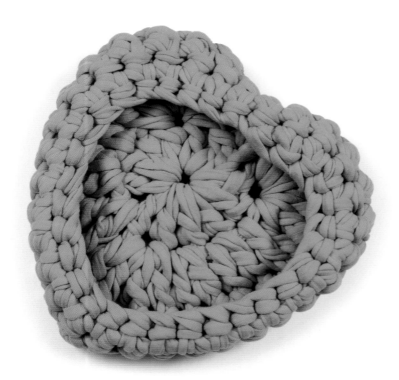

## Instructions:

Make an adjustable ring, ch 3 and work 12 dc *(UKtr)* into ring, sl st to top of 3-ch (13 sts). Gently pull the yarn tail to close the ring.

Round 1: miss 2 sts, 7 tr *(UKdtr)* in next st, 1 dc *(UKtr)* in next st, 2 dc *(UKtr)* in each of the next 2 sts, [1 dc *(UKtr)*, 1 ch, 1 tr *(UKdtr)*, 1 ch, 1 dc *(UKtr)*] in next st to make the point of the heart, 2 dc *(UKtr)* in each of the next 2 sts, 1 dc *(UKtr)* in next st, 7 tr *(UKdtr)* in next st, sl st into first missed st.

Round 2: 1 ch, sc *(UKdc)* in each st to bottom of heart, 3 sc *(UKdc)* in next st, sc *(UKdc)* in each st to end.

Rounds 3–4: 1 ch, sc *(UKdc)* in each st around, sl st into initial ch.

Fasten off, weave in all loose ends.

# Valentine

## Materials:

Rowan handknit cotton in red (A) and white (B)

1 x 50g/85m/93yd

## Tools:

US size 6/4mm crochet hook

## Notions:

1 heart-shaped red button

## Finished size:

From bottom point to centre top between lobes: 4in (10cm)

## Instructions:

Using yarn A, ch 10, sc *(UKdc)* in second ch from hook to end (9 sts).

Rows 1–9: 1 ch, sc *(UKdc)* to end. This makes a square.

### To make the right lobe:

Row 10: 1 ch, 9 tr *(UKdtr)* into centre st of one side of square, sl st to corner.

### To make left lobe (working along the next straight edge):

Row 11: 1 ch, 9 tr *(UKdtr)* into centre st of next side of square, sl st to corner.

Row 12: sc *(UKdc)* down one edge of the square and up the other side, stopping at the start of the tr *(UKdtr)* sts, sl st to join.

Fasten off.

Row 13: Join yarn B to the middle of the two lobes and sc *(UKdc)* around. Work two sc *(UKdc)* into one st at the centre of each lobe, and into the st at the bottom point, work 1 sc *(UKdc)*, 1 hdc *(UKhtr)*, 1 sc *(UKdc)*; sl st into middle of lobes to finish.

Fasten off and weave in all loose ends.

### To make the flower:

Using yarn B, ch 4, sl st to first ch to form a ring.

Round 1: 1 ch, sc *(UKdc)* in ring ten times, sl st to ch-1 to join.

Round 2: [2 ch, 2 dc *(UKtr)*, 1 hdc *(UKhtr)*] in first st, sl st to next st, *1 hdc *(UKhtr)*, 2 dc *(UKtr)*, 1 hdc *(UKhtr)* in next st, sl st in next st, rep from * three times, sl st to first st to join.

Fasten off.

### Making up:

Position the button centrally over the flower and attach them to the centre of the heart through the button, using yarn A.

Fasten off and weave in all loose ends.

# Coasters

## Materials:

Small amounts of Rowan Handknit Cotton in variations of pale blue (A) and navy (B) or variations of these plus cream and mid-blue

1 x 50g/85m/93yd

## Tools:

US size 6/4mm crochet hook

## Finished size:

From bottom point to centre top between lobes: 4½in (11cm)

## Instructions:

Using yarn A, ch 2, work 3 sc (UKdc) in second ch from hook (3 sts).

Row 1: 1 ch, 1 sc (UKdc) in each st (3 sts).

Row 2: 1 ch, 2 sc (UKdc) in first st, 1 sc (UKdc), 2 sc (UKdc) into last st (5 sts).

Row 3: 1 ch, 2 sc (UKdc) in first st, 3 sc (UKdc), 2 sc (UKdc) into last st (7 sts).

Row 4: 1 ch, sc (UKdc) into each st (7 sts).

Row 5: 1 ch, 2 sc (UKdc) in first st, 5 sc (UKdc), 2 sc (UKdc) into last st (9 sts).

Row 6: 1 ch, sc (UKdc) into each st (9 sts).

Row 7: 1 ch, 2 sc (UKdc) into first st, 7 sc (UKdc), 2 sc (UKdc) into last st (11 sts).

Row 8: 1 ch 1, sc (UKdc) into each st (11 sts).

Row 9: 1 ch, 2 sc (UKdc) into first st, 9 sc (UKdc), 2 sc (UKdc) into last st (13 sts).

Row 10: 1 ch, 2 sc (UKdc) into first st, 11 sc (UKdc), 2 sc (UKdc) into last st (15 sts).

Row 11: 1 ch, 2 sc (UKdc) into first st, 13 sc (UKdc), 2 sc (UKdc) into last st (17 sts).

Rows 12 and 13: 1 ch 1, sc (UKdc) into each st (17 sts).

Row 14: 1 ch, 2 sc (UKdc) in first st, 15 sc (UKdc), 2 sc (UKdc) in last st (19 sts).

Row 15: 1 ch 1, sc (UKdc) into each st (19 sts).

Row 16: 1 ch, 2 sc (UKdc) in first st, 17 sc (UKdc), 2 sc (UKdc) in last st (21 sts).

Row 17: 1 ch, sc (UKdc) into each st (21 sts).

### To make right lobe of heart:

Row 18: 1 ch, 10 sc (UKdc), turn (10 sts).

Row 19: 1 ch, sc (UKdc)2tog, sc (UKdc) in each st (9 sts).

Row 20: 1 ch, sc (UKdc)2tog, sc (UKdc) to last 2 sts, sc (UKdc)2tog (7 sts).

Row 21: 1 ch, sc (UKdc)2tog, sc (UKdc) to last 2 sts, sc (UKdc)2tog (5 sts).

Row 22: 1 ch, sc (UKdc)2tog, sc (UKdc) to last 2 sts, sc (UKdc)2tog (3 sts).

Fasten off.

### To make left lobe of heart:

Row 23: Rejoin yarn A to tenth st from left (there will be one unworked st in the middle), 1 ch, 10 sc (UKdc), turn (10 sts).

Row 24: 1 ch, sc (UKdc) to last 2 sts, sc (UKdc)2tog (9 sts).

Row 25: 1 ch, sc (UKdc)2tog, sc (UKdc) to last 2 sts, sc (UKdc)2tog (7 sts).

Row 26: 1 ch, sc (UKdc)2tog, sc (UKdc) to last 2 sts, sc (UKdc)2tog (5 sts).

Row 27: 1 ch, sc (UKdc)2tog, sc (UKdc) to last 2 sts, sc (UKdc)2tog (3 sts).

Fasten off.

### Edging:

Join yarn B to the right of the bottom point, ch 1, sc (UKdc) in each st around. You may need to work 2 sc (UKdc) into one or two sts on the curves of the heart lobes so that the yarn is not too tight. At the bottom point, work [1sc (UKdc), 1hdc (UKhtr), 1 sc (UKdc)] into the centre st, sl st to initial ch.

Fasten off and weave in all loose ends.

# Heart String

## Materials:

Small amounts of Rowan pure wool DK in maroon, pink and mushroom, 1 x 50g ball/130m/142yd

Sewing thread

Toy stuffing

## Tools:

US size 6/4mm crochet hook

Sewing needle

## Notions:

8 small bell beads

3 hanging decorations in toning colours

## Finished size:

23¼in (59cm) from top of loop to bottom of hanging decoration

## Instructions (make 2 for each heart):

Round 1: With yarn colour of your choice, make an adjustable ring, ch 3, and work into the ring 6 sc *(UKdc)*, 1 dc *(UKtr)*, 6 sc *(UKdc)*, 3ch, sl st. Gently pull the tail end of the yarn to close the ring (but leave a small gap, as your final sl st will be made into the centre) and the heart shape will appear.

Round 2: 3 ch, miss the 3-ch from previous round, 3 sc *(UKdc)* into the first st, 1 sc *(UKdc)* in each of the next 2 sts, 1 hdc *(UKhtr)* in each of the next 3 sts, [1 dc *(UKtr)*, 1 tr *(UKdtr)*, 1 dc *(UKtr)*] into the next st (this is the bottom point of the heart), 1 hdc *(UKhtr)* in each of the next 3 sts, 1 sc *(UKdc)* in each of the next 2 sts, 3 sc *(UKdc)* in the last st, ch 3 and sl st in the centre of the heart.

### Edging:

First, tug the yarn tail again to make sure the centre hole is closed properly, as you will now be stuffing the heart. This will prevent any toy stuffing poking through.

Holding two hearts tog with WS facing, join yarn to the right of the bottom point, ch 1 and sc *(UKdc)* in each st through both layers. You may need to work 2 sc *(UKdc)* into one or two sts on the curves of the heart lobes so that the stitches do not pull. At the bottom point of the heart, work 1 sc *(UKdc)*, 1 dc *(UKtr)*, 1 sc *(UKdc)* into the middle st, then sl st into initial ch. Fasten off and weave in all loose ends.

### Making up:

Choose a colour for the hanging chain and connect the six hearts tog by joining yarn to the middle of the heart lobes, make 6 ch and join to bottom point of next heart. Repeat to join all hearts tog. To make the hanging loop, join yarn to the middle of the heart lobes on the top heart, make 16 ch and rejoin to the middle. Fasten off.

Sew a bell bead to the bottom of the top five hearts, and three to the bottom of the last heart. Attach some hanging decorations with gold and maroon beads to the bottom heart with some yarn.

16

# Earrings and Pendant

**Materials:**

Small amount of DMC Petra No. 3 in pink

1 x 100g ball/280m/306yd

**Tools:**

US size 1.5/2.5mm crochet hook

2 x jewellery pliers

**Notions:**

3 heart-shaped silver hoops

2 ear wires

3 jump rings

Chain with clasp

## Instructions (make 3):

Attach yarn to heart-shaped hoop, ch 1 and
sc (*UKdc*) all around, keeping sts as neat as
possible. Make sure you have worked enough
sts to conceal the silver heart and sl st into
initial ch. Fasten off and weave in loose ends.

### Making up:

For all three hearts, attach one jump ring to the
centre stitch between the heart lobes. Attach
an earwire to two of the jump rings to complete
the earrings. For the remaining heart, thread
the chain through the jump ring to complete
the pendant.

# Brooch

## Materials:

Small amount of Rowan Pure Wool DK in mushroom (A), 1 x 50g ball/130m/142yd

Small amount of Drops Kid Silk in heather (B), 1 x 25g ball/200m/219yd

Small piece of thin pink felt

Pale pink yarn

## Tools:

US size 6/4mm crochet hook

US size C or D/3mm crochet hook

Sewing needle

## Notions:

Approx. 50 pale pink seed beads

3 large pale pink pearl beads

Brooch back

## Finished size:

From bottom point to centre top between lobes 2¾in (7cm)

## Instructions:

Using yarn A, make an adjustable ring, ch 3 and work 7 dc (UKtr) in ring, ss into top of 3-ch and pull yarn tail to close the hole (8 sts).

Round 1: 2 ch, hdc (UKhtr) in same st, 2 hdc (UKhtr) in each st around sl st to top of 2 ch (16 sts).

Round 2: 2 ch, 1 hdc (UKhtr) in each st around, sl st to top of 2-ch (16 sts).

Round 3: 1 ch, [1 sc (UKdc), 1 hdc (UKhtr), 1 dc (UKtr), 1 tr (UKdtr)] in next st, 4 tr (UKdtr) in next st, 3 tr (UKdtr) in next st, 3 dc (UKtr) in next st, [1 dc (UKtr), 1 hdc (UKhtr)] in next st, 2 hdc (UKhtr) in next st, [1 hdc (UKhtr), 1 dc (UKtr)] in next st; [1 dc (UKtr), 1 tr (UKdtr), 1 dc (UKtr)] in centre bottom st.

This completes the left half of the heart; now continue round 3 by reversing these sts for the right side:

[1 dc (UKtr), 1 hdc (UKhtr)] in next st, 2 hdc (UKhtr) in next st, [1 hdc (UKhtr), 1 dc (UKtr)] in next st, 3 dc (UKtr) in next st, 3tr (UKdtr) in next st, 4 tr (UKdtr) in next st, [1 tr (UKdtr) in next st, 1 dc (UKtr), 1 hdc (UKhtr), 1 sc (UKdc)], in next st, 1 ch, sl st to initial ch.

## Flower:

Using yarn B and US size 3/3mm crochet hook, ch 26.

Row 1: sc (UKdc) in second ch from hook, sc (UKdc) to end (25 sts).

Row 2: 1 ch, *miss 1 st, 5 dc (UKtr) in next st, sl st in next st, rep from * to last st, sl st into last st.

Fasten off, leaving a long tail of yarn, curve the length of crochet round into a flower shape (see photograph for guidance) and secure it with a few stitches. Attach it to the centre of the heart with the yarn tail and fasten off. Using the sewing needle and pale pink sewing thread, attach the pale pink seed beads to the edges of the petals. Then attach the three large beads to the centre of the flower.

## Making up:

Using the sewing needle and thread, attach a rectangular piece of doubled thin felt to the back of the brooch with blanket stitch, then sew the brooch back to the felt.

# Pincushion

## Materials:

Small amounts of DMC Petra No. 3 yarn in pink in dark pink (A), pale green (B) and pale pink (C)

1 x 100g ball/280m/306yd

Small amount of toy stuffing

## Tools:

US size 4/3.5mm crochet hook

## Finished size:

From bottom point to centre top between lobes: 3½in (9cm)

## Instructions:

Using yarn A, make an adjustable ring, ch 2, 7 hdc (UKhtr), sl st to top of 2-ch (8 sts).

Round 1: 2 ch, 1 hdc (UKhtr) in same st, 2 hdc (UKhtr) in each stitch around, sl st to top of 2-ch (16 sts).

Round 2: 2 ch, 1 hdc (UKhtr) in each st around, sl st to top of 2-ch (16 sts).

Round 3: 1 ch, [1 sc (UKdc), 1 hdc (UKhtr), 1 dc (UKtr), 1 tr (UKdtr)] in next st, 4 tr (UKdtr) in next st, 3 tr (UKdtr) in next st, 3 dc (UKtr) in next st, [1 dc (UKtr), 1 hdc (UKhtr)] in next st, 2 hdc (UKhtr) in next st, [1 hdc (UKhtr), 1 dc (UKtr)] in next st; [1 dc (UKtr), 1 tr (UKdtr), 1 dc (UKtr)] in centre bottom st.

This completes the left half of the heart; now continue round 3 by reversing these sts for the right side:

[1 dc (UKtr), 1 hdc (UKhtr)] in next st, 2 hdc (UKhtr) in next st, [1 hdc (UKhtr), 1 dc (UKtr)] in next st, 3 dc (UKtr) in next st, 3 tr (UKdtr) in next st, 4 tr (UKdtr) in next st, [1 tr (UKdtr) in next st, 1 dc (UKtr), 1 hdc (UKhtr), 1 sc (UKdc)] in next st, 1 ch, ss to initial ch.

Fasten off.

Round 4: Join yarn B to first st, 1 ch, sc (UKdc) into next four sts, 2 sc (UKdc) in each of next 2 sts, sc (UKdc) to bottom point of heart; into middle st at the bottom point, work [1 sc (UKdc), 1 hdc (UKhtr), 1 sc (UKdc)], sc (UKdc) up right side to last 6 sts, 2 sc (UKdc) in each of next 2 sts, sc (UKdc) to end, sl st into first ch.

Round 5: 2 ch, hdc (UKhtr) into back loop only of each st to bottom point of heart, work [1 sc (UKdc), 1 hdc (UKhtr), 1 sc (UKdc)] in next st, hdc (UKhtr) into back loop only of each st to end, sl st into top of 2-ch.

Fasten off and weave in all loose ends.

### Edging:

With both hearts WS together, join yarn C to centre of heart lobes, 1 ch, sc (UKdc) in each st around to bottom point of heart, working through both layers. You may need to work 2 sc (UKdc) into one or two sts around the curve of the heart lobes so that the stitches do not pull. Begin stuffing the heart at this point, and continue stuffing as you work around until the heart is quite plump; take care not to stuff it too tightly, otherwise the stuffing will poke through the stitches. At bottom point of the heart, work [1 sc (UKdc), 1 hdc (UKhtr), 1 sc (UKdc)] into the centre st, then continue working sc (UKdc) into each st around to the top, sl st into first ch.

Fasten off and weave in loose ends.

# Snowflakes

## Materials:

DMC Petra No. 5 in various
colours (A) and white (B)

## Tools:

US size C or D/3mm crochet hook

## Finished size:

2³/₈in (6cm) at widest point

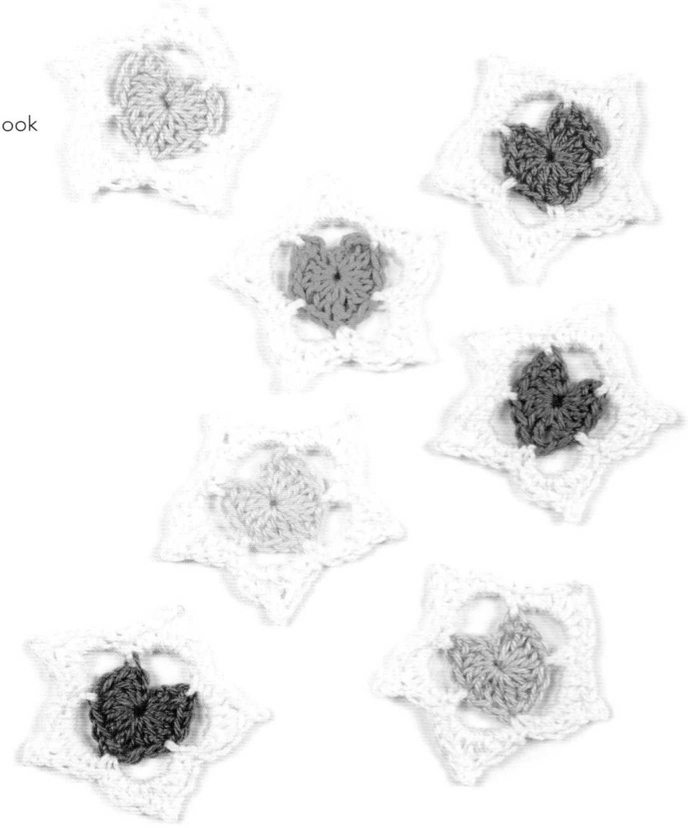

## Instructions:

### To make the heart:

Round 1: Using yarn A,
ch 4, 5 dc (UKtr) in fourth
ch from hook, 1 ch, 1 tr
(UKdtr), 1 ch, 5 dc (UKtr), 3
ch, sl st in centre (13 sts).
Fasten off.

### To make the snowflake points:

Round 2: Join yarn B to bottom point of
heart with sl st, 5 ch, miss 2 sts and sl st into
third st, 5 ch, miss 2 sts and sl st into third st
(at top right lobe of heart), 5 ch, sl st into top of 3 ch (at top
left lobe of heart), 5 ch, miss 2 sts and sl st into third st, 5 ch
and sl st into bottom point of heart.

Round 3 (working into the first 5-ch space): *1 ch, 1 sc
(UKdc), 2 hdc (UKhtr), 1 dc (UKtr), 1 ch, sl st into top of dc
(UKtr) just worked, 2 hdc (UKhtr), 1 sc (UKdc), sl st into next
5-ch*; rep from * to * into each 5-ch sp, ending with a ss
into initial 1 ch.

Fasten off and weave in all loose ends.

Block as desired.

# Lavender Heart

## Materials:

1 x 50g ball of DMC Natura Just
  Cotton in lavender (A) and a
  small amount of green (B)

1 x 50g ball/155m/170yd

Sewing thread

Toy stuffing

Dried lavender

## Notions:

Pearl bead

## Tools:

US size 4/3.5mm crochet hook

Sewing needle

## Finished size:

From bottom point to centre
top between lobes: 2¾in (7cm)

## Instructions (make 2):

Using yarn A, ch 3 and make 1 turning ch.

Row 1: 1 sc (UKdc) in second ch from hook, 2 sc
(UKdc) (3 sts).

Row 2: 1 ch, 2 sc (UKdc) in first st, sc (UKdc) in
second st, 2 sc (UKdc) in last st (5 sts).

Row 3: 1 ch, 2 sc (UKdc) in first st, sc (UKdc) to
last st, 2 sc (UKdc) in last st (7 sts).

Row 4: 1 ch, 2 sc (UKdc) in first st, sc (UKdc) to
last st, 2 sc (UKdc) in last st (9 sts).

Row 5: 1 ch, 2 sc (UKdc) in first st, sc (UKdc) to
last st, 2 sc (UKdc) in last st (11 sts).

Row 6: 1 ch, sc (UKdc) across (11 sts).

Rows 7–9: 1 ch, 2 sc (UKdc) in first and last sts
and sc (UKdc) in between (17 sts).

Row 10: 1 ch, sc (UKdc) across (17 sts).

Row 11: 1 ch, 2 sc (UKdc) in first st, sc (UKdc) to
last st, 2 sc (UKdc) in last st (19 sts).

Row 12: 1 ch, sc (UKdc) across (19 sts).

Row 13: 1 ch, 2 sc (UKdc) in first st, sc (UKdc) to
last st, 2 sc (UKdc) in last st (21 sts).

Rows 14 and 15: 1 ch, sc (UKdc) across (21 sts).

To make right lobe of the heart:

Row 16: 1 ch, 10 sc (UKdc), turn.

Row 17: 1 ch, sc (UKdc)2tog, sc (UKdc) to end
(9 sts).

Rows 18-20: 1 ch, sc (UKdc)2tog, sc (UKdc) to
last 2 sts, sc (UKdc)2tog (3 sts).

Fasten off.

### To make the left lobe of the heart:

Row 21: Rejoin yarn to the st next to middle st
(middle st will remain unworked) and work 10
sc (UKdc).

Row 22: 1 ch, sc (UKdc) to last 2 sts, sc
(UKdc)2tog (9 sts).

Rows 23–25: as rows 18–20.

Fasten off and weave in all loose ends.

### Making up:

With both hearts together, join yarn A to the
middle of the heart lobes, work 1 ch and sc
(UKdc) around the edge, working 2 sts every
so often in the same place at the curve of the
lobes, and 3 sc (UKdc) in the bottom point of
the heart to accentuate the shape. Start stuffing
the heart when you are halfway round the edge,
placing a small amount of dried lavender in the
very centre, then continue stuffing as you work.
Join the last st to first ch with a sl st and
fasten off.

Weave in loose end.

### Flower:

Using yarn A, ch 26, sc (UKdc) in second ch from
hook and sc (UKdc) to end (25 sts).

Row 1: 1 ch, *miss 1 st, 5 hdc (UKhtr) into next
st, sl st into next st*, rep to end of row ending
with a sl st.

Fasten off with a long tail of yarn, curve the
length of crochet round into a flower shape and

secure it with a few stitches. Attach it to the centre of the heart with the yarn tail and fasten off. Sew the pearl bead to the centre with the sewing needle and thread.

### Leaves (make 2):

With yarn B, ch 8.

Row 1: 1 sc (UKdc) in second chain from hook, 1 hdc (UKhtr), 1 dc (UKtr), 2 dc (UKtr) in next ch, 1 dc (UKtr), 1 hdc (UKhtr), 1 sc (UKdc), 2 ch, sl st in second ch from hook to make picot point.

Now work a 'mirror image' of row 1 along the bottom of the foundation chain into the single loops.

Row 2: 1 sc (UKdc), 1 hdc (UKhtr), 1 dc (UKtr), 2 dc (UKtr) in next ch, 1 dc (UKtr), 1 hdc (UKhtr), 1 sc (UKdc), sl st into the last ch.

Fasten off, leaving a long tail.

Pin the leaves into position just under the bottom of the flower and, using the long yarn tail, attach them securely to the heart with a few stitches underneath so that they do not show.

### Hanging loop:

Attach yarn A to the middle of the heart lobes with a sl st, ch 16 and join with a sl st to the middle again. Fasten off and weave in loose ends.

# Nautical Heart

## Materials:

Small amount of thick, recycled cotton

1 x skein 14m/15yd; 1 x 1000g spool 140m/153yd

## Tools:

US size 16/12mm crochet hook

Large-eyed needle

## Notions:

21 large blue wooden beads

## Finished size:

From bottom of tail to centre top between lobes: 23in (58cm)

## Instructions:

Ch 11, sc *(UKdc)* in second ch from hook to end (10 sts).

Rows 1–10: 1 ch, sc *(UKdc)* to end. This section will be a square.

### To make the first lobe of the heart:

Row 11: *1 ch, 1 trtr *(UKqtr)* into centre st along edge of last row*, rep 8 times, sl st to next corner.

### To make the second lobe of the heart:

Row 12: *1 ch, 1 trtr *(UKqtr)* into centre of next side of square*, rep 8 times, sl st to next corner.

Fasten off yarn and weave in ends.

### Making up:

To add beads to the lobes of the heart, thread a long length of yarn onto a large-eyed needle and attach to the right side of the lobe.

Push the needle in between the third and fourth stitches from the edge and thread a bead onto the needle (the bead will sit in the 1-ch space between the stitches), then push the needle through to the next ch-sp and repeat. Add five beads in this way, then push the needle through to the top of the heart, threading on four beads and leaving a long length for hanging. Push the needle back down into the heart, missing the first two stitches and continue to complete the left lobe of the heart. Weave in the loose end securely and cut yarn.

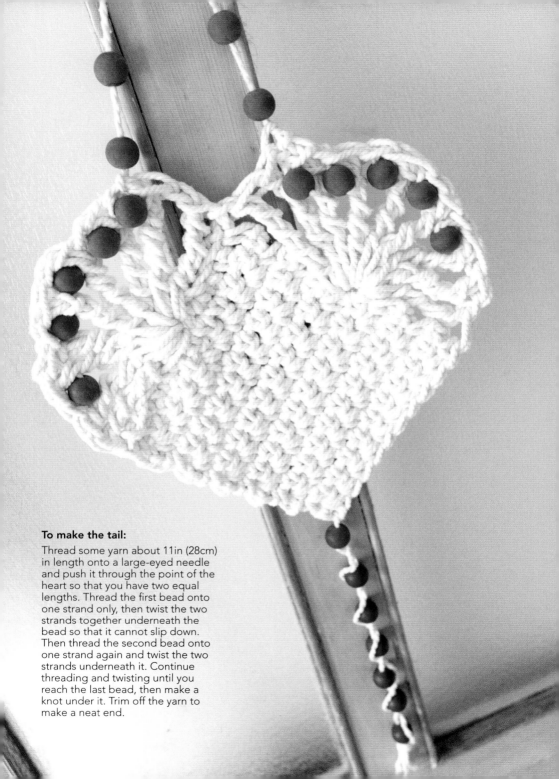

**To make the tail:**

Thread some yarn about 11in (28cm) in length onto a large-eyed needle and push it through the point of the heart so that you have two equal lengths. Thread the first bead onto one strand only, then twist the two strands together underneath the bead so that it cannot slip down. Then thread the second bead onto one strand again and twist the two strands underneath it. Continue threading and twisting until you reach the last bead, then make a knot under it. Trim off the yarn to make a neat end.

# Bookmark

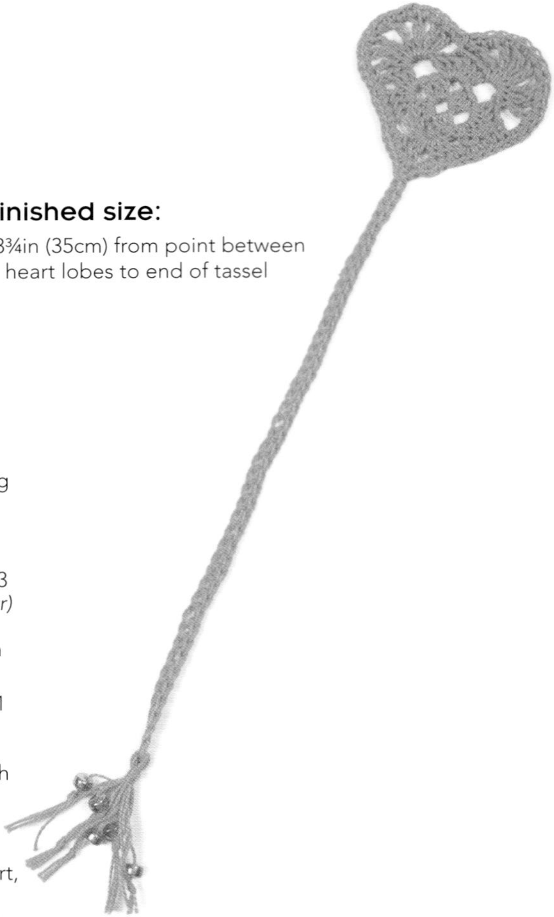

## Materials:

Small amount of Petra DMC 5 in kingfisher

1 x 100g/400m/437yd

## Tools:

US size 1.5/2.5mm crochet hook

## Notions:

5 small turquoise beads

## Finished size:

13¾in (35cm) from point between heart lobes to end of tassel

## Instructions:

Ch 5 and join with a sl st to make a ring.

Round 1: Ch 3 (counts as first dc (UKtr)), 2 dc (UKtr) into ring, 2 ch, [3 dc (UKtr), 2 ch] into ring three more times. Join with a sl st to top of beginning 3-ch (12 dc (UKtr), four 2-ch sps).

Round 2: Sl st in next 2 sts and into 2-ch sp, 3 ch (counts as first dc (UKtr)), [2 dc (UKtr), 2 ch, 3 dc (UKtr)] in 2-ch sp, 2 ch, *miss next 3 dc (UKtr) and work 3 dc (UKtr), 2 ch, 3 dc (UKtr) in next 2-ch sp, 2 ch;* rep from * to * twice more; join with a sl st to initial 3-ch.

Round 3: Sl st in next 2 sts and into 2-ch sp; *1 ch, 1 dc (UKtr) into next 2-ch sp (centre of the square), 1 ch, [1 dc (UKtr), 1 ch] six more times in same 2-ch space, join with a sl st in next 2-ch sp*. One lobe of the heart is now completed. Rep from * to * to make second lobe. Fasten off.

Round 4: Rejoin yarn at the bottom of the heart, just to the right of the point, make 1 ch, and sc (UKdc) round into sts and ch-sps, working 2 sc (UK dc) into the 2-ch sp. At the dip between the two heart lobes, make a sl st in the middle, then continue in sc (UKdc). At the bottom point of the heart, work 1 sc (UKdc), 1 dc (UKtr), 1 sc (UKdc) into the point and finish with a sl st into the first ch at beg of round.

Fasten off and weave in all loose ends.

### To make the tail:

Rejoin yarn at the bottom point of the heart and make 35 ch, sc (UKdc) into second st from hook and sc (UKdc) to end, sl st back to point and fasten off.

### To make the tassel:

Wind a length of yarn round your four fingers held together nine or ten times and cut the end. Now cut through the loops at one end and thread through a tapestry needle. Push the needle through the bottom of the tail and pull so that the yarn is even on both sides. Tie another length of yarn round the top, just below the end of the tail, to secure the top of the tassel. Now thread some small blue beads onto several threads so that they hang at different heights and tie a knot below the beads to secure them. Block the heart and tail if desired.

# Rug

## Materials:

1 x ball grey jersey yarn and small amount of lime green jersey yarn for edging;1200g/120m/131yd

## Tools:

US size 16/12mm crochet hook

Large-eyed needle

## Finished size:

From bottom point to centre top between lobes: 14½in (37cm)

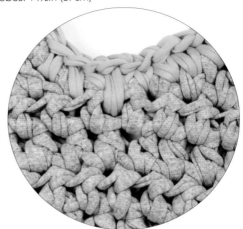

## Instructions:

Row 1: Ch 2, 3 hdc *(UKhtr)* in 2nd ch (3 sts).

Row 2: Ch 2, 1 hdc *(UKhtr)* in each st (3 sts).

Row 3: Ch 2, 2 hdc *(UKhtr)* in first st, 1 hdc *(UKhtr)* in next st, 2 hdc *(UKhtr)* in last st (5 sts).

Row 4: Ch 2, 2 hdc *(UKhtr)* in each of the next two sts, hdc *(UKhtr)* in each st to last two, 2 hdc *(UKhtr)* in each of the last two sts (9 sts).

Rows 5, 9 and13: continue working as row 3, starting with ch 2, working 2 hdc *(UKhtr)* in first and last st, and single hdc *(UKhtr)* in the stitches between, so that you are increasing by 2 sts per row.

Rows 6, 8 and 11: Continue working as row 4, starting with ch 2, working 2 hdc *(UKhtr)* in each of the first two and last two stitches and single hdc *(UKhtr)* in the stitches between, so that you are increasing by 4 sts per row.

Rows 7, 10 and 12: Ch 2, work 1 hdc *(UKhtr)* in each st across.

You will have 27 sts at end of row 13.

Row 14: Ch 2, hdc *(UKhtr)* 2tog, 9 hdc *(UKhtr)*, hdc *(UKhtr)*2tog, turn (11 sts).

Row 15: Ch 2, hdc *(UKhtr)* 2tog, 7 hdc *(UKhtr)*, hdc *(UKhtr)*2tog, turn (9 sts).

Row 16: Ch 2, hdc *(UKhtr)* 2tog, 5 hdc *(UKhtr)*, hdc *(UKhtr)*2tog, turn (7 sts).

Row 17: Ch 2, hdc *(UKhtr)* 2tog, 3 hdc *(UKhtr)*, hdc *(UKhtr)*2tog, turn (5 sts).

Row 18: Ch 2, hdc *(UKhtr)* 2tog, hdc *(UKhtr)*, hdc *(UKhtr)*2tog (3 sts).

Fasten off.

Row 19: Rejoin yarn to 13th st from left on row 13, leaving 1 st in the middle unworked; hdc *(UKhtr)* 2tog, 9 hdc *(UKhtr)*, hdc *(UKhtr)* 2tog, turn (11 sts).

Rows 20–23: work as rows 15–18, then fasten off.

### Edging

Join lime green yarn to the stitch on the right of the bottom point of the heart, ch 1 and sc *(UKdc)* around the edge, making your stitches as even as possible. You will be working into row ends, so you may have to force the hook into the yarn at some points. Make 1 long stitch in the middle of the heart lobes to accentuate the shape. When you reach the bottom point of the heart, into the middle stitch work 1 sc *(UKdc)*, 1 hdc *(UKhtr)*, 1 sc *(UKdc)*, then sl st into the initial ch-1. Fasten off and weave in all loose ends with the large-eyed needle.

Jersey yarns have different amounts of 'stretch', so do not expect your finished item to be a perfect shape; part of the charm of this yarn is its slightly bumpy finish.

# Heart Charm

## Materials:

Small amounts of Rowan Handknit Cotton in blue (A), pink (B) and pale blue (C), 1 x 50g/85m/93yd

Small amount of toy stuffing

## Tools:

US size 6/4mm crochet hook

## Notions:

2 small pink heart-shaped buttons

2 small silver heart-shaped beads

Lobster clasp

## Finished size:

8in (20cm) from top of key ring charm to bottom of tail

## Crab stitch:

With RS of work facing, working from left to right, insert hook in next stitch to the right. Yarn over, draw yarn through stitch. Yarn over, draw yarn through 2 loops on hook (1 crab st completed).

## Instructions (make 2):

Using yarn A, ch 10, sc (UKdc) in second ch from hook, sc (UKdc) in each ch to end (9 sts).

Rows 1–9: 1 ch, sc (UKdc) to end. This makes a square.

### To make right lobe of heart:

Row 10: 1 ch, 9 tr (UKdtr) into centre st along last row, sl st to corner.

### To make left lobe of heart (working along the next straight edge):

Row 11: 1 ch, 9 tr (UKdtr) into centre st, sl st to next corner.

Row 12: 1 ch, sc (UKdc) down one edge of square to bottom point of heart, work into centre st [1 sc (UKdc), 1 hdc (UKhtr), 1 sc (UKdc)], continue in sc (UKdc) to where you started, sl st into initial ch.

Fasten off.

### Chain stitch decoration:

On the RS of one heart, using yarn C, work ch st in a heart shape, using the photograph as a guide, and sew one button to the top of the chain stitch heart.

### Flower:

Using yarn B, ch 4, sl st to first ch to form a ring.

Round 1: 1 ch, sc (UKdc) in ring ten times, sl st to ch-1 to join.

Round 2: [2 ch, 2 dc (UKtr), 1 hdc (UKhtr)] in first st, sl st in next st, *1 hdc (UKhtr), 2 dc (UKtr), 1 hdc (UKhtr) in next st, sl st in next st from*, rep three times, sl st to first st to join.

Fasten off, leaving a long yarn tail, and use this to attach a button and the flower to the heart. Fasten off and weave in loose ends.

### Crab stitch edging:

Holding WS together, join yarn B to the middle of the heart lobes, 1 ch and work crab stitch (working from left to right) around to the bottom point. Make 3 sts into the centre st to accentuate the point, then continue round to the middle of the heart lobes and sl st to initial ch.

Fasten off and weave in all loose ends.

### Beaded tail:

Attach a length of yarn B to the bottom point of the heart, double it over and thread both strands through one bead. Make a knot under the bead, thread both strands through the second bead and knot again. Cut off the excess yarn.

### To make the loop:

Join yarn B to the middle of the lobes with a sl st, ch 20, sl st in second ch from hook and in each st to the end. Cut a long yarn tail and thread the loop through bottom of the lobster clasp. Join end of yarn to the middle of the lobes, secure and weave in loose end.

# Long Tall Heart

## Materials:

1 x 50g ball of Rowan handknit cotton in green (A)
  and small amount of ecru (B), 50g/85m/93yd

Small amount of toy stuffing

## Tools:

US size 6/4mm crochet hook

## Finished size:

From bottom point to centre top
between lobes: 7½in (19cm)

## Instructions:

For this heart, ch 1 and turn your work at the
end of each row.

### Pattern (make two)

Ch 2 (counts as a st) 1 sc *(UKdc)* in second ch
from hook.

Row 1: 1 sc *(UKdc)* in each st (2 sts).

Row 2: 1 sc *(UKdc)* in each st (2 sts).

Row 3: 2 sc *(UKdc)* in first st, 1 sc *(UKdc)* (3 sts).

Row 4: 1 sc *(UKdc)* in each st (3 sts).

Row 5: 1 sc *(UKdc)*, 2 sc *(UKdc)* in middle st, 1 sc
*(UKdc)* (4 sts).

Row 6: 1 sc *(UKdc)* in each st (4 sts).

Row 7: 2 sc *(UKdc)* in first st, sc *(UKdc)* in next 3
sts (5 sts).

Row 8: 1 sc *(UKdc)* in each st (5 sts).

Row 9: 2 sc *(UKdc)* in first st, sc *(UKdc)* in next 3
sts, 2 sc *(UKdc)* in last st (7 sts).

Rows 10 and 11: 1 sc *(UKdc)* in each st (7 sts).

Row 12: 2 sc *(UKdc)* in first st, sc *(UKdc)* in next 5
sts, 2 sc *(UKdc)* in last st (9 sts).

Rows 13–15: 1 sc *(UKdc)* in each st (9 sts).

Row 16: 2 sc *(UKdc)* in first st, sc *(UKdc)* in next 7
sts, 2 sc *(UKdc)* in last st (11 sts).

Rows 17–19: 1 sc *(UKdc)* in each st (11 sts).

Row 20: 2 sc *(UKdc)* in first st, sc *(UKdc)* in next 9
sts, 2 sc *(UKdc)* in last st (13 sts).

Rows 21–23: 1 sc *(UKdc)* in each st (13 sts).

Row 24: 2 sc *(UKdc)* in first st, sc *(UKdc)* in next
11 sts, 2 sc *(UKdc)* in last st (15 sts).

Rows 25–27: 1 sc *(UKdc)* in each st (15 sts).

Row 28: 2 sc *(UKdc)* in first st, sc *(UKdc)* in next
13 sts, 2 sc *(UKdc)* in last st (17 sts).

Rows 29–31: 1 sc *(UKdc)* in each st (17 sts).

### To make the heart lobes:

Continue to ch 1 and turn your work at the end
of each row.

### Right lobe:

Row 32: 1 sc *(UKdc)* in next 8 sts (8 sts). Leave
the rest of this row unworked and turn.

Row 33: As row 32.

Row 34: sc *(UKdc)*2tog, sc *(UKdc)* in next 4 sts,
sc *(UKdc)*2tog (6 sts).

Rows 35 and 36: 1 sc *(UKdc)* in each st (6 sts).

Row 37: sc *(UKdc)*2tog, sc *(UKdc)* in next 2 sts,
sc *(UKdc)*2tog (4 sts).

Row 38: sc *(UKdc)*2tog, sc *(UKdc)*2tog (2 sts).

Fasten off.

### Left lobe:

Rejoin yarn A to the stitch on the left of the
middle stitch on row 31.

Rows 39 and 40: 1 sc *(UKdc)* in each st (8 sts).

Row 41: sc *(UKdc)*2tog, sc *(UKdc)* in next 4 sts,
sc *(UKdc)*2tog (6 sts).

Rows 42 and 43: 1 sc *(UKdc)* in each st (6 sts).

Row 44: sc *(UKdc)*2tog, sc *(UKdc)* in next 2 sts, sc *(UKdc)*2tog (4 sts).

Row 45: sc *(UKdc)*2tog, sc *(UKdc)*2tog (2 sts).

Fasten off and weave in all loose ends.

### Making up

With WS together, join yarn B immediately to the right of the bottom point of the heart, ch 1 and sc *(UKdc)* through both hearts evenly up the side and round the right lobe to the centre. Start stuffing the heart at this point, and add more when you are halfway round to the bottom point so it is quite taut. For the centre dip between the heart lobes, make 3 sc *(UKdc)* so you do not lose the shape, then continue to sc *(UKdc)* around. At the bottom point of the heart, in the middle stitch, work 1 sc *(UKdc)*, 1hdc *(UKhtr)*, 1 sc *(UKdc)* to accentuate the point, then ss into initial chain. Fasten off and weave in the loose end. Attach yarn B to the middle of the lobes, ch 20 to form a hanging chain, join to middle lobes and fasten off. Weave in loose ends.

# Sweetheart Hair Clip

## Materials:

Small amounts of Rowan handknit cotton in
pale green (A) and pink (B)

1 x 50g/85m/93yd

Sewing thread

## Tools:

US size 4/3.5mm crochet hook

Sewing needle

## Notions:

Snap hair clip

## Finished size:

From bottom point to centre top between
lobes: 1¾in (4.5cm)

## Instructions:

Round 1: Using yarn A, make an adjustable ring and work 5
dc *(UKtr)*, 1 ch, 1 tr *(UKdtr)*, 1 ch, 5 dc *(UKtr)*, all into the ring
and sl st into the ring. Pull the yarn tail to close the ring and
the heart shape will reveal itself.

Fasten off.

Round 2: Join yarn B to top of L lobe and sc *(UKdc)* in each
st round to bottom point of heart; in centre st, work 1 sc
*(UKdc)*, 1 dc *(UKtr)*, 1 sc *(UKdc)* to accentuate the point and
continue to work in sc *(UKdc)* round to the R lobe, sl st in
centre and sl st into first sc *(UKdc)*.

Fasten off and weave in all loose ends.

Block if desired.

### Making up:

Using a sewing needle and matching thread, sew the snap
to the back of the heart lengthways.

### Opposite

*This pretty hair clip can be made for a
child or an adult. Simply use a larger
snap hair clip for an adult and either
work a second edging round if you
want to make the heart a little larger,
or use thicker yarn.*

# Christmas Decoration

## Materials:

Patons Diploma Gold DK in red (A) and green (B); 1m/1yd metallic silver thread (C), 1 x 50g ball/120m/131yd

Green sewing thread

## Tools:

US size 6/4mm crochet hook

Sewing needle

## Notions:

A few small silver and green beads

## Finished size:

From bottom point to centre top between lobes: 4¾in (12cm)

## Instructions:

### Make two:

Using yarn A, ch 40, join with a sl st in first ch, do not twist the chain.

Round 1: Ch 3 (counts as first dc (UKtr)), 2 dc (UKtr) in the same st, 1 dc (UKtr) in each of the next 10 ch, 2 dc (UKtr) in each of the next 7 ch, (yo, insert hook in next ch and pull up a loop, yo and pull through 2 loops on hook) five times, yo and pull through all 6 remaining loops on hook, 2 dc (UKtr) in each of the next 7 ch, 1 dc (UKtr) in each of the next 10 ch, 2 dc (UKtr) in the same st as the first dc (UKtr); join with a sl st in the top of the beginning 3-ch.

### The tree (make two):

Using yarn B, ch 2 (counts as a st), 2 sc (UKdc) in second ch from hook (2 sts).

Row 1: 1 ch, 2 sc (UKdc) in each st (4 sts).

Row 2: 1 ch, 2 sc (UKdc) in first st, 1 sc (UKdc) in next 2 sts, 2 sc (UKdc) in last st (6 sts).

Rows 3 and 4: 1 ch, 1 sc (UKdc) in each st.

Row 5: 1 ch, 2 sc (UKdc) in first st, sc (UKdc) in next four sts, 2 sc (UKdc) in last st (8 sts).

Fasten off.

Row 6: Rejoin yarn B to fourth st, 1 ch (counts as a st), 1 sc (UKdc) in next st (2 sts).

Rows 7–9: 1 ch, 1 sc (UKdc) in each st.

Fasten off.

Use yarn ends to attach the tree to the centre of the red heart by its three points and the bottom of the trunk.

Pin and block the two pieces carefully with starch.

### Making up:

With WS together, join yarn C to the right of bottom point of heart, 1 ch and sc (UKdc) through both layers all around. At the bottom point of the heart, work 1 sc (UKdc), 1 hdc (UKhtr), 1 sc (UKdc) to accentuate the point, sl st to initial ch.

Fasten off, weave in all loose ends.

Attach the beads randomly to both sides of the tree with the sewing needle and thread.

To make the hanger, attach yarn A to the top centre of the right lobe, ch 20 and sl st to top centre of left lobe. Fasten off and weave in loose end.

# Granny Square Table Mat

## Materials:

Small amounts of Rowan Handknit
Cotton in red (A), ecru (B), dark blue
(C), rust (D) and light blue (E)

1 x 50g/85m/93yd

## Tools:

US size 6/4mm crochet hook

## Finished size:

From bottom point to centre top
between lobes: 9in (23cm)

## Instructions:

Using yarn A, make an adjustable ring, 3 ch
(counts as a st), 11 dc (UKtr) into ring, join with
sl st to top of 3-ch (12 sts). Fasten off.

Round 1: Join yarn B to a space between sts,
4 ch (counts a first dc (UKtr) and 1 ch), then work
1 dc (UKtr) and 1 ch into each space between
sts (12 dc (UKtr) and 12 1-ch sps), join with a sl st
to 3rd chain of first 4 ch. Fasten off.

Round 2: Join yarn C into a 1-ch sp, 3 ch (counts
as a st), 2 dc (UKtr); *3 ch, 3 dc (UKtr) into next
ch sp, rep from * to end, 3 ch, join with sl st into
top of initial 3-ch to join.

Round 3: Join yarn D to a 3-ch sp, 3 ch counts
as a st), 3 dc (UKtr) into same 1-ch sp; *2 ch, 4
dc (UKtr), rep from * to end, 2 ch, sl st in top of
initial 3-ch to join.

Round 4: Join yarn E to any 2 ch sp, 1 ch, 1 dc
(UKtr) into same ch sp, 1 ch; [3 dtr (UKtrtr), 3 ch,
3 dtr (UKtrtr), 1 ch] into next ch sp; 3 tr (UKdtr),
1 ch into next ch sp; [3 dc (UKtr), 1 ch] into next
3 ch sps; [1 tr (UKdtr), 2 dtr (UKtrtr), 3 ch, 2 dtr
(UKtrtr), 1 tr (UKdtr), 1 ch] into next ch sp to
form the point of the heart; [3 dc (UKtr), 1 ch]
into next 3 ch sps; [3 tr (UKdtr), 1 ch] into next
ch sp; [3 dtr (UKtrtr), 3 ch, 3 dtr (UKtrtr), ch 1] in

next ch sp; [1 dc (UKtr), 1 sc (UKdc)] into next ch
sp. Join with a sl st to first ch. Fasten off.

Round 5: Join yarn C to first ch sp to left of
centre dip, work [2 sc (UKdc), 1 hdc (UKhtr), 1
ch] into this space; [3 dc (UKtr), 1 ch, 1 dc (UKtr),
1 tr (UKdtr), 1 dtr (UKtrtr), 1 ch] into next ch
sp; [5 dtr (UKtrtr), 1 ch] into next ch sp; [1 dtr
(UKtrtr), 1 tr (UKdtr), 1 dc (UKtr), 1 ch] into next
ch sp; [3 dc (UKtr), 1 ch] into next 3 ch sps; [3 dc
(UKtr), 2 ch, 3 dc (UKtr), 1 ch] into next ch sp;
[3 dc (UKtr), 1 ch] into next 3 ch sps; [1 dc (UKtr),
1 tr (UKdtr), 1 dtr (UKtrtr), 1 ch] into next ch sp;
[5 dtr (UKtrtr), 1 ch] into next ch sp;
[1 dtr (UKtrtr), 1 tr (UKdtr), 1 dc (UKtr), 1 ch,
3 dc (UKtr), 1 ch] into next ch sp; [1 hdc (UKhtr),
2 sc (UKdc)] into last ch sp; sc (UKdc) into sts
in middle of heart, sl st to first sc (UKdc) at
beginning of round.

Round 6: Join yarn A to any st, sc (UKdc) fairly
loosely in each st around; at the bottom point
of heart, work into the middle st [1 sc (UKdc),
1 hdc (UKhtr), 1 sc (UKdc)], to accentuate the
point, then continue to sc (UKdc) to end, sl st to
the first sc (UKdc).

Fasten off and weave in all loose ends.

Block as desired.

# Filet Heart

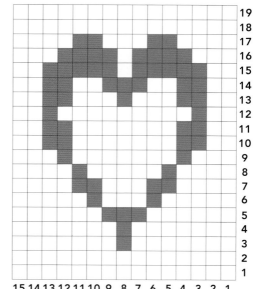

## Materials:

Small amount of Petra DMC No. 5 crochet
cotton, in pink (53805), 100g/400m/437yd

## Tools:

US size 1.5/2.5mm crochet hook

## Finished size:

8in (20.5cm)

## Note:

To work filet crochet, make a multiple of 3 ch
for each mesh square, plus 5 extra to make
the right-side edge and the top of the first
mesh square of the first row. To make a filet
block, instead of working 2 chains to make
an empty mesh square, work 2 trebles to fill
in the square.

## Instructions:

Ch 47.

Row 1: 1 sc (UKdc) in eighth ch from hook, *2
ch, miss next 2 ch, 1 sc (UKdc) in next ch; rep
from * to end, turn.

Row 2: 5 ch, miss first st, 1 sc (UKdc) in next st,
*2 ch, 1 sc (UKdc) in next st; rep from * working
last sc (UKdc) in third ch from last sc (UKdc) in
row below.

Follow the chart, making filet blocks in the
coloured squares to form the heart shape. You
will have two rounds of mesh filet at the edges.
Fasten off.

### Scallop edging

Rejoin yarn in one of the 2-ch sps and work
[sl st, hdc (UKhtr), dc (UKtr), hdc (UKhtr)] in each
2-ch space around. In the corner spaces, work:
sl st, sc (UKdc), hdc (UKhtr), 3 dc (UKtr), hdc
(UKhtr), sc (UKdc), sl st. Fasten off and weave in
all loose ends. Pin the finished filet heart
out carefully and block using starch for the
best finish.

# Mug Hug

## Materials:

1 x ball of Debbie Bliss Baby Cashmerino in green (A) and a small amount of pink (B), 1 x 50g ball/125m/137yd

## Tools:

US size 4/3.5mm crochet hook

## Notions:

Large plastic button

## Finished size:

To fit a mug with a circumference of 9¾in (24.5cm)

## Instructions:

Using yarn A, ch 35, hdc *(UKhtr)* in third ch from hook, hdc *(UKhtr)* to end (33 sts).

Rows 1–6: Ch 2, hdc *(UKhtr)* in each st.

Fasten off.

### Edging:

With rectangle laid lengthways, attach yarn B just above the bottom R corner, ch 1 and sc *(UKdc)* all the way round, making 3 sc *(UKdc)* in each corner st. Sl st into the initial ch and then sl st to the third st up the R side, 30 ch, sc *(UKdc)* in second ch from hook, sc *(UKdc)* in each ch to end, and cut a long tail of yarn. Attach the loop 3 sts down from the top and fasten off.

Weave in all loose ends.

### Heart (make two):

Round 1: Using yarn A, make an adjustable ring, ch 1, 9 sc *(UKdc)* in the ring, sl st to initial first st (9 sts).

Round 2: 1 ch, [1 sc *(UKdc)*, 1 hdc *(UKhtr)*, 1 dc *(UKtr)*] in next st, 2 dc *(UKtr)* in next st, [1 dc *(UKtr)*, 1 hdc *(UKhtr)*] in next st, 2 sc *(UKdc)* in next st, [1 hdc *(UKhtr)*, 1 dc *(UKtr)*, 1 hdc *(UKhtr)*] in middle st, 2 sc *(UKdc)* in next st, [1 hdc *(UKhtr)*, 1 dc *(UKtr)*] in next st, 2 dc *(UKtr)* in next st, [1 dc *(UKtr)*, 1 hdc *(UKhtr)*, 1 sc *(UKdc)*] in next st, sl st to initial ch.

### Edging:

Join yarn B to the middle of the two lobes, ch 1, sc *(UKdc)* in each st around. You may need to work 2 sc *(UKdc)* into one or two sts on the curves of the heart lobes so that the stitches do not pull. At the bottom point, work [1 sc *(UKdc)*, 1 hdc *(UKhtr)*, 1 sc *(UKdc)*] into the centre st, continue working in sc *(UKdc)* to end, sl st to initial ch.

Fasten off and weave in all loose ends.

### Making up:

Wrap the hug round your mug and mark the point where the button should go. Attach the button with yarn B, then position the hearts evenly across the rectangle and attach them with small stitches underneath so they do not show at the front.

*It is easy to adjust this mug hug to fit the mug of your choice. Simply make the foundation chain and check that it fits round your mug, leaving space for the button loop. You can make it longer too if you want to use it on a tall mug.*

## Publisher's Note

If you would like to learn more about crochet, try *Crochet for the Absolute Beginner* by Pauline Turner, Search Press, 2014.

## Acknowledgements

My thanks to Coats, Texere Yarns, DMC and Cygnet Yarns for providing some of the lovely yarns for these projects, and to Marrianne Miall, Winifred's Daughter of Hawkhurst and Sue Stratford for providing some of the notions.
Thanks to Katie French at Search Press for giving me this opportunity and to Sophie Kersey for her expert editorial skills.
Thanks also to Fiona Murray for the beautiful photography.
Finally, thanks to my family – Simon, Tom, Zoe and Anna – for their encouragement, and for putting up with my ever-exploding yarn stash migrating around the house.